The Science of Living Things

What is a Life Cycle?

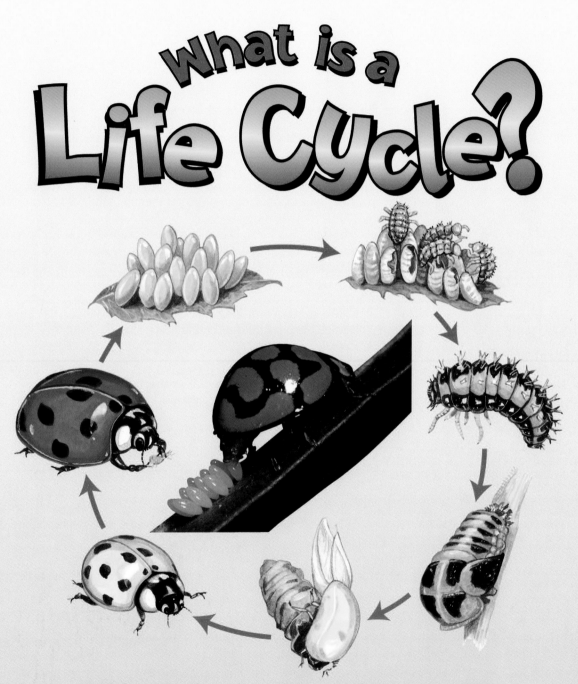

Bobbie Kalman & Jacqueline Langille

 Crabtree Publishing Company

www.crabtreebooks.com

The Science of Living Things Series
A Bobbie Kalman Book

For funky, spunky Valerie

Editor-in-Chief
Bobbie Kalman

Writing team
Bobbie Kalman
Jacqueline Langille

Managing editor
Lynda Hale

Editors
Niki Walker
Greg Nickles

Computer design
Lynda Hale
McVanel Communications Inc.
(cover concept)

Production coordinator
Hannelore Sotzek

Consultant
K. Diane Eaton, Hon.
B.Sc., B.A.,
Brock University

Special thanks to
The Hale family, who appears on page 5

Photographs
Gary Barton: page 5 (bottom)
Bob Cranston/Mo Yung Productions: page 19 (bottom)
Bobbie Kalman: page 31 (all)
Diane Payton Majumdar: page 20 (bottom right)
Photo Researchers, Inc.: Alan & Sandy Carey: page 23; Michael P. Gadomski:
    page 6; Tom McHugh: page 25; Dr. Paul A. Zahl: page 19 (bottom left)
James H. Robinson: page 9
Tom Stack & Associates: David G. Barker: page 16; Jeff Foott: page 18
(bottom);   Denise Tackett: page 19 (top); Joe McDonald: page 15 (top);
John Canalosi:
    page 15 (middle); David M. Dennis: page 15 (bottom)
Kenneth Thomas: page 8
Valan Photos: Jeff Foott: page 18 (top both); V. Wilkinson: page 22
Jerry Whitaker: page 20 (left center)
Other photographs by Digital Stock and Digital Vision

Illustrations
All illustrations by Barbara Bedell except the following:
    Antoinette "Cookie" Bortolon: page 14

Crabtree Publishing Company
www.crabtreebooks.com   1-800-387-7650

Printed in Canada/032020/EN20200214

Library of Congress Cataloging in Publication Data
Kalman, Bobbie
    What is a life cycle?
(The science of living things)
Includes index.
ISBN 0-86505-874-1 (library bound)   ISBN 0-86505-886-5 (pbk.)
This book introduces the life cycles of plants, insects, amphibians, reptiles,
fish, birds, mammals, including humans, and discusses birth, growth,
parental care, and reproduction.

1. Life cycles (Biology)—Juvenile literature. [1. Animal life cycles. 2. Life
cycles (Biology)] I. Title. II. Series: Kalman, Bobbie. Science of living things.
QH501.K255 1998   j571.8   LC 98-2560
                                                                        CIP

Published in Canada
Crabtree Publishing
616 Welland Ave.
St. Catharines, Ontario
L2M 5V6

Published in the United States
Crabtree Publishing
PMB 59051
350 Fifth Avenue, 59th Floor
New York, New York 10118

Published in the United Kingdom
Crabtree Publishing
Maritime House
Basin Road North, Hove
BN41 1WR

Published in Australia
Crabtree Publishing
3 Charles Street
Coburg North
VIC, 3058

Contents

What is a life cycle?

This frog is an adult. When the frog has offspring, a new life cycle begins.

Every living thing has a **life cycle**. A life cycle is all the stages a living thing goes through between the time it is born and the time it becomes an adult. All life cycles have the same basic stages—being born, growing, and changing into an adult.

Growing and changing

All living things grow and change during their life cycles. Their bodies grow and change on the outside and inside. When the changes are complete, the **organism**, or single living thing, is an adult. Adult plants make **seeds**. When an animal is an adult, its body is ready to make **offspring**, or young.

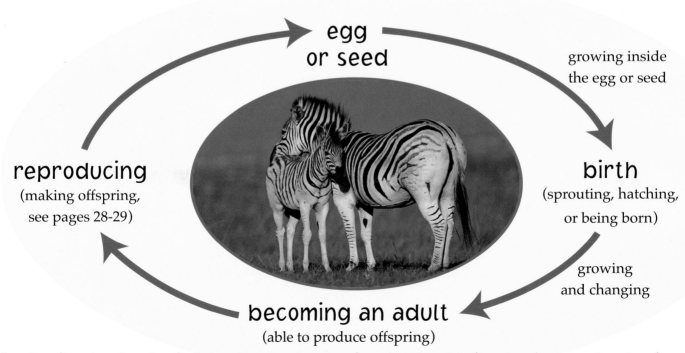

egg
or seed

growing inside
the egg or seed

reproducing
(making offspring,
see pages 28-29)

birth
(sprouting, hatching,
or being born)

growing
and changing

becoming an adult
(able to produce offspring)

The cycle starts again

When an adult makes offspring, another life cycle begins. The offspring goes through the same life cycle stages as its parents until it too becomes an adult. The offspring may then have young of its own and begin a new life cycle.

Keeping the species alive

A **species**, or type of plant or animal, survives only when enough of adults continue the life cycle by making offspring. If a species of plant or animal stops **reproducing**, or making offspring, it dies out.

*(below) A human family has different **generations**—grandparents, parents, and children. The family continues with each new generation. If the children in a family do not have children of their own some day, the family will not continue after they die.*

(above) Many trees grow blossoms that become fruit. The fruit contains the seeds that start a new life cycle.

Plants and their seeds

Most plants begin their life cycle as a seed. Inside each seed is a tiny baby plant, or **embryo**. A seed also contains food for the embryo to use as it grows.

A tough covering, called a **seed coat**, keeps the embryo from drying out. An embryo starts to grow when it has enough warmth, water, and **nutrients**.

*Seeds do not always begin growing right after they fall to the ground. Some baby plants stay **dormant**. A dormant seed waits for the right amount of water and sunshine before it starts to grow.*

6

The life cycle of a plant

Not all plants grow from seeds, but most do. The pictures below show the life cycle of a bean plant. It starts and ends with a seed.

*1. When a seed **germinates**, or starts to grow, its seed coat breaks. The embryo then sends out roots and a stem.*

*2. A baby plant, or **seedling**, uses the stored food in the seed to grow leaves. A plant needs leaves to make food for itself.*

3. If the seedling gets enough water and sunlight, it grows into an adult plant with many leaves.

6. The plant drops its seeds. They may grow into new plants. The life cycle then starts again.

5. As the seeds grow, they are protected in pods.

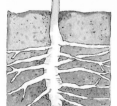

4. An adult plant grows flowers to make the seeds that will start the next life cycle.

Many kinds of eggs

In most life cycles, new life begins inside an egg. All animals, including fish, birds, and insects, start out inside an egg. The female adults of each species make eggs inside their bodies. Different animals produce different types of eggs. For example, bird eggs have hard shells, but fish and frog eggs are covered in jelly.

turtle eggs hatching

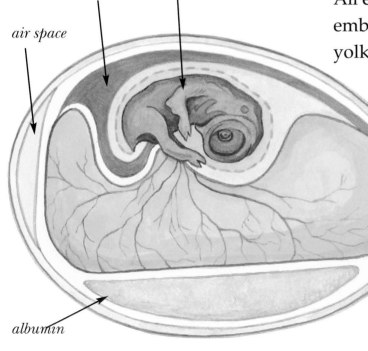

air space

allantois   *embryo*

albumin

What's in an egg?

All eggs contain an embryo and a **yolk**. The embryo is the growing baby animal. The yolk is food that is stored for the embryo to use as it grows. Eggs have an outer layer such as a shell or thick jelly that protects the embryo.

shell

yolk sac

An egg is the perfect home for a growing embryo. The hard shell of this bird egg keeps the baby moist and protected. The **albumin***, or egg white, acts as a cushion. The* **allantois** *absorbs waste from the embryo.*

Laying eggs

Most animals **lay** their eggs, or push them out of their bodies. Some animals keep their eggs inside their bodies until the babies hatch. Others such as mammals, have eggs that are not covered in a tough shell or jelly. This type of egg grows in a special part of its mother's body until it becomes a baby that is ready to be born.

*Only a few types of animals guard their eggs after they are laid. This wolf spider carries her **egg case** on her body for weeks. After hatching, her **spiderlings**, or baby spiders, climb onto her back and hitch a ride for a few days.*

Metamorphosis

Metamorphosis is a major part of the life cycle of some animals, including frogs, toads, newts, and many insects. Metamorphosis is the change that happens to an animal's body structure and habits as it grows into an adult. Before young animals go through metamorphosis, they look very different from their parents. They usually eat different foods as well.

Metamorphosis helps a species survive because the young live in a different environment and do not have to compete with the adults for food. For example, a butterfly baby, or **larva**, eats leaves and crawls to move around. After metamorphosis, shown opposite, the adult flies from plant to plant to find its new food, which is usually **nectar**, the sweet juice inside flowers.

The life cycle of a newt

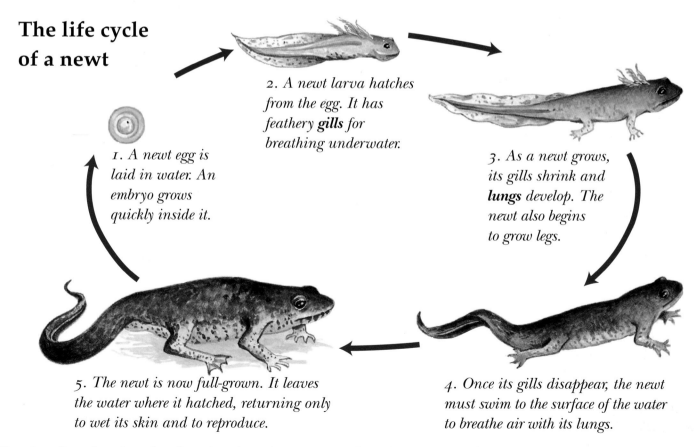

*2. A newt larva hatches from the egg. It has feathery **gills** for breathing underwater.*

1. A newt egg is laid in water. An embryo grows quickly inside it.

*3. As a newt grows, its gills shrink and **lungs** develop. The newt also begins to grow legs.*

5. The newt is now full-grown. It leaves the water where it hatched, returning only to wet its skin and to reproduce.

4. Once its gills disappear, the newt must swim to the surface of the water to breathe air with its lungs.

The life cycle of a butterfly

1. An adult female butterfly lays her eggs on a leaf and then flies away.

2. A larva hatches from an egg. Many insect larvae look like worms. Butterfly larvae are also called **caterpillars**. *They constantly munch on leaves.*

3. A full-grown caterpillar spins a case called a **cocoon** *around itself. The larva is now called a* **chrysalis**.

4. Inside the cocoon, the body changes in many ways until it becomes an adult. The newly formed butterfly breaks through the cocoon and flies away.

The life cycle of arthropods

Arthropods are animals that have an **exoskeleton**. An exoskeleton is a hard covering that protects an animal's body like a suit of armor. Insects, arachnids, myriapods, and crustaceans such as crabs and lobsters are arthropods.

Almost all arthropods lay eggs to begin a new life cycle. A female usually lays her eggs near a food supply. A nearby food source is important because most parents leave their eggs, and the babies must be able to find food on their own.

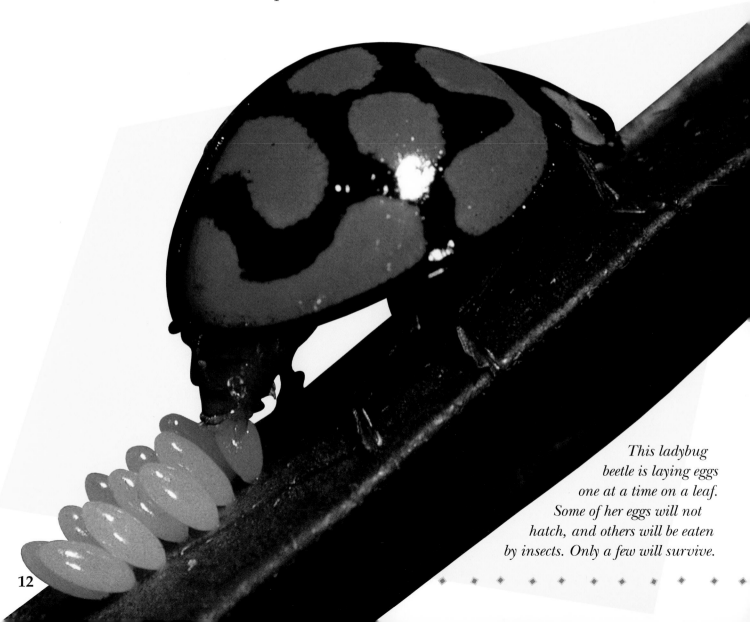

This ladybug beetle is laying eggs one at a time on a leaf. Some of her eggs will not hatch, and others will be eaten by insects. Only a few will survive.

The life cycle of ladybug beetles

The life cycle of a ladybug beetle is only four to seven weeks long! In that short time, a ladybug hatches, grows, goes through metamorphosis, and then makes offspring of its own.

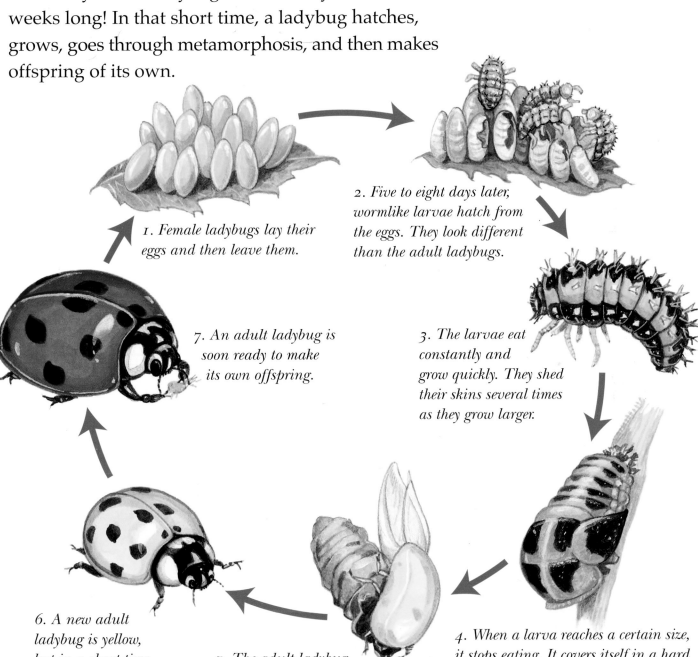

1. Female ladybugs lay their eggs and then leave them.

2. Five to eight days later, wormlike larvae hatch from the eggs. They look different than the adult ladybugs.

3. The larvae eat constantly and grow quickly. They shed their skins several times as they grow larger.

7. An adult ladybug is soon ready to make its own offspring.

6. A new adult ladybug is yellow, but in a short time its exoskeleton changes to red.

5. The adult ladybug breaks the shell and spreads its wings for the first time.

*4. When a larva reaches a certain size, it stops eating. It covers itself in a hard shell and is called a **pupa**. Inside the shell, it changes to an adult.*

An amphibian's life cycle

Frogs, toads, salamanders, newts, and caecilians are **amphibians**. The name "amphibian" means "double life." Most amphibians spend the early part of their lives underwater and then live on land as adults. Most amphibian larvae, called **tadpoles**, look very different from their parents. They live underwater and breathe with gills. Tadpoles eat plants and use their long tails to swim. During metamorphosis, a tadpole grows lungs and legs, and its tail shrinks. Once it is an adult, an amphibian mainly lives on land and eats insects.

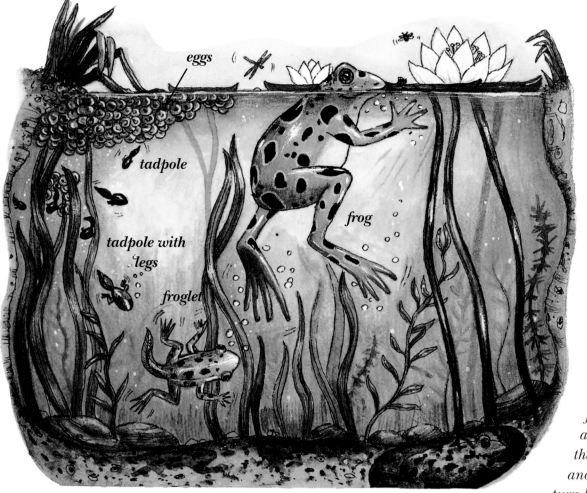

eggs

tadpole

tadpole with legs

froglet

frog

*Frogs lay large numbers of eggs, called **spawn**. Animals eat many frog eggs, but a few survive. If a tadpole hatches, it is still in great danger of being eaten. Only a few eggs ever become adult frogs. (To see the life cycle of a newt, another amphibian,* *turn back to page 10.)*

(left) Adult amphibians, such as this salamander, need clean, fresh water in which to lay their eggs.

(below) A large adult great crested newt shares the same pond as a larva. The small larva breathes underwater through gills on the sides of its head.

The water of life

The life cycle of amphibians depends on water at every stage. Most types of amphibians lay their jelly-covered eggs in water. The eggs must stay wet or the embryos inside dry out and die. A tadpole can only breathe underwater using gills in the same way fish do. Adult amphibians need water, damp air, or moist soil to keep their skin from becoming too dry. Most amphibians spend their entire life cycle in or near water.

A young spotted salamander leaves the water for the first time.

Life as a reptile

*When a baby reptile hatches, it is in great danger from **predators**, which are animals that eat other animals. Many reptiles die before they are a year old. Scientists raise some types of reptiles to help them survive.*

Reptiles are animals that have leathery skin covered with scales. Lizards, snakes, turtles, tortoises, crocodiles, alligators, and tuataras are reptiles. Many types live on land, but turtles, crocodiles, and alligators spend most of their lives in water. Most reptiles begin their life cycles in eggs.

Carbon copies

When reptile babies hatch, they are tiny copies of their parents. They are called **hatchlings**. Hatchlings do not go through metamorphosis because they already have the same body shapes as adult reptiles. To survive as adults, however, they must grow much larger and stronger.

*A turtle hatchling's shell is softer than an adult's shell. As the turtle grows, its shell becomes harder. Its body makes new shell layers, called **growth rings**, so that the shell always fits.*

Outgrowing their skin

As most reptiles grow, the outer layer of their skin does not, and they soon outgrow it. Many young lizards and snakes must **molt**, or shed, their skin more than four times a year. Some adult reptiles molt only once or twice a year. Adult reptiles continue to grow slowly and molt their skin. They do not stop growing and molting until they die.

Many baby reptiles molt a short time after they hatch.

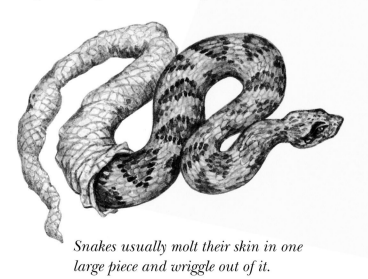

Snakes usually molt their skin in one large piece and wriggle out of it.

Lizards shed their skin in several small pieces. Their scales do not come off when they lose their skin.

≈ Living underwater ≈

Most fish are egg-laying animals that spend their entire life cycles underwater. They live in oceans, lakes, and rivers. A female lays her eggs in the water. A male **fertilizes** the eggs by spreading **sperm** over them. Most fish leave their eggs alone. Birds and other fish feed on the unguarded eggs. Many types of fish lay hundreds or thousands of eggs at one time because only a few survive and grow into adults. When a baby fish hatches, it is called a larva or **fry**.

1. These fish eggs have tiny salmon growing inside. The baby salmon at the top of the picture is hatching. The other fry is only a few seconds old.

2. Many types of fry have an attached yolk sac that they use for food as they grow. By the time the yolk is almost gone, the fry is able to find food on its own.

3. Very few fry survive to become adults. If a fry is not eaten by predators, it grows into an adult fish within one year after hatching.

Fish life

Not all fish lay eggs and then leave them. Some parents protect their young from predators. A few build nests in the sand for their eggs. Sometimes one parent guards the eggs constantly until they hatch.

(below) A male seahorse holds the female's eggs in a special pouch until they hatch. A tiny baby is coming out of its father's pouch.

(above) A mouth brooder holds its eggs in its mouth until they hatch.

(below) Sharks do not guard their eggs, but shark eggs have a tough egg case. An egg case protects the baby better than a jelly covering does.

The life cycle of birds

ostrich guarding its eggs

Birds live all over the world. Most live on land, but some species, such as ducks and sea gulls, spend much of their time on water. All birds return to land to lay their eggs, however. Many fly great distances to find nesting areas where there is plenty of food for their **chicks**, or babies.

Brooding and hatching

Many birds **brood** their eggs once they are laid. Brooding is sitting over eggs to keep them warm. The embryo inside the egg needs warmth to grow properly.

When a chick is big enough to hatch, it scratches on the inside of the eggshell. It has an egg-tooth on the end of its beak to help it break the shell. After a few hours, the tired baby wriggles out, as shown below. A new life cycle begins!

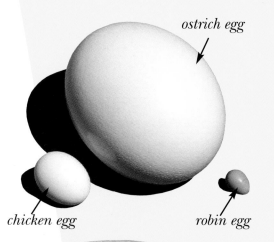

ostrich egg

chicken egg

robin egg

The embryo grows quickly inside the egg. Soon the baby bird has no room to move.

Caring for their young

Most birds do not lay many eggs at once. They must be careful parents in order to make sure their young survive. Birds guard their eggs and chicks from predators and protect them from rain and too much sun. They feed their chicks until they are old enough to leave the nest.

Some birds care for their chicks even after they leave the nest. They help their young find the right food and show them how to escape or hide from predators. Many birds are fully grown a year after they hatch and are ready to start their own family.

(right) One type of chick hatches blind, helpless, and almost naked. Songbirds have this kind of chick.

The other type of chick is open-eyed and covered in soft feathers. A few hours after these chicks hatch, their parents lead them out of the nest.

Life as a mammal

A mammal's life cycle is different from the life cycle of other animals in two important ways—birth and feeding. Most mammals grow inside their mothers' bodies where they are well protected. When they are large enough to come into the world, they are **live born**, as shown below. A live-born animal is born alive from its mother's body instead of hatching from an egg.

After birth, most animals have to feed themselves, but mother mammals make milk in their bodies to feed their babies. A baby drinks milk from its mother's body. From its mother's milk, a young mammal gets all the nutrients it needs to grow properly.

This farmer is helping one of his sheep as she gives birth. The baby lamb is born alive from its mother's body.

Weaning away from milk

As a baby grows older, it starts to eat solid foods because its mother does not let it drink as much milk. When it is ready to eat only adult food, it is **weaned**, which means it no longer drinks milk from its mother's body.

*This cougar is **nursing**, or feeding milk to, her cubs. Mother mammals usually wait patiently while their babies are drinking.*

Ensuring the life cycle

The offspring of plants and most animals must be able to survive on their own. Many mammal species, however, care for their young after they are born. The extra care parents give their babies helps more of them survive. Mammals do not need to have many young at once to ensure their species will continue.

Teaching survival skills

Parents that care for their young teach them how to survive. Young animals learn which foods to eat and where to find water to drink. Some meat-eaters such as lions spend weeks showing their young how to hunt and catch **prey**, as shown below. Prey are animals that predators eat.

Licking their offspring is a way for parents to place their own scent on their babies. The scent tells other adult animals to whom the young belong.

The human life cycle

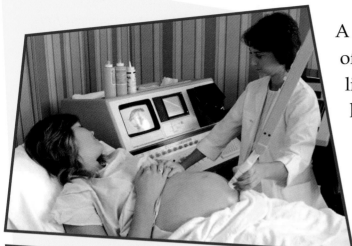

A human life cycle is similar to the life cycle of other mammals. Every healthy human is live born, grows, and becomes an adult. A human begins life as an embryo and then grows into a baby inside its mother's body.

Checking on the embryo

Many humans take special care of their children before they are born. A doctor checks the baby with an **ultrasound examination**, as shown in the top left photograph. An ultrasound machine shows a picture of the baby while he or she is inside his or her mother's body. The doctor checks the picture to see if the baby is growing properly.

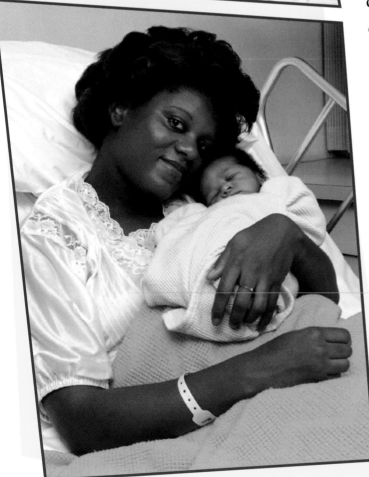

Caring for a child

Many animals can walk and feed themselves soon after they are born, but a newborn human baby is helpless. Human babies need their parents to provide them with food, warmth, and protection. They also need to be held and comforted by their parents.

The life cycle of a human

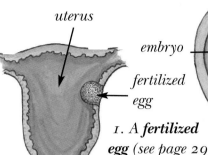

uterus

embryo

fertilized
egg

*1. A **fertilized egg** (see page 29) begins the life cycle in an organ called the **uterus**.*

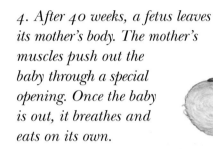

*2. A human egg grows into an embryo with the **placenta**.*

placenta

*3. A human embryo receives nourishment from its mother's body through the placenta and **umbilical cord**. After eight weeks of growing and changing, the embryo is called a **fetus**.*

umbilical
cord

4. After 40 weeks, a fetus leaves its mother's body. The mother's muscles push out the baby through a special opening. Once the baby is out, it breathes and eats on its own.

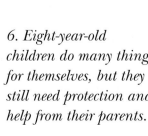

8. Human adults are fully grown. They are able to have babies of their own.

5. By the time a child is three years old, he or she can usually walk, run, and talk in simple sentences.

6. Eight-year-old children do many things for themselves, but they still need protection and help from their parents.

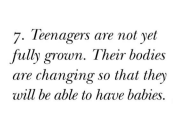

7. Teenagers are not yet fully grown. Their bodies are changing so that they will be able to have babies.

Keeping the cycle going

Every living thing is created through reproduction. Reproduction is the way plants and animals make offspring. Living things reproduce in different ways. Every species needs offspring because the adults do not live forever. Without reproduction and offspring, a species becomes **extinct**, or disappears.

*To make offspring, some simple creatures split in half. **Amoebas** are tiny living things that divide in half to reproduce. Each new amoeba then starts a life cycle by itself.*

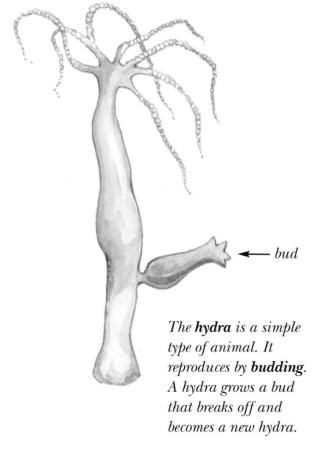

← *bud*

*The **hydra** is a simple type of animal. It reproduces by **budding**. A hydra grows a bud that breaks off and becomes a new hydra.*

spores →

*Mushrooms are a type of **fungus**. Many types of fungi reproduce with **spores**. Each tiny, dustlike spore can become a new mushroom.*

Joining sperm and eggs

Only a few living things simply split in half to reproduce. Most species reproduce when a male's sperm fertilizes a female's **ovum**, or egg cell. When a sperm and an ovum join together, they create a fertilized egg.

pistil (where egg cells grow)

stamens covered with pollen

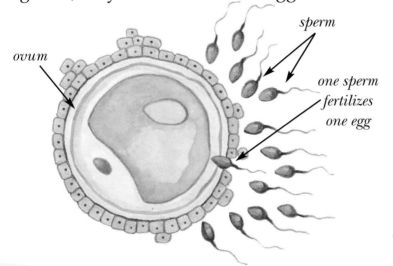

ovum

sperm

one sperm fertilizes one egg

*Most plants need sperm and eggs to reproduce. Many types make sperm and **ovules**, or egg cells, inside flowers. The tiny, dustlike sperm are called **pollen**. When pollen from one plant fertilizes another plant's ovule, a seed is formed.*

*(below) Most male and female animals **mate** in order to bring the male's sperm and the female's egg cells together inside the female's body.*

(above) After these male and female millipedes mate, they will have hundreds of offspring, but only a few will survive to continue the species.

Dangers to life cycles

A life cycle for a species ends when all its members die and no offspring are alive to keep the cycle going. Predators, **pollution**, and people can each cause the end of a life cycle for a plant or an animal. If a species becomes extinct, the life cycles of other species are harmed as well. Every life cycle depends on at least one other life cycle to continue.

All animals need other animals or plants for food. If polluted water kills the frogs in a certain pond, the frog-eating predators must find food in a new place. If all the frogs in the world are killed, however, those frog-eating predators also become extinct because they have no food. Two life cycles end when one species dies out.

The life cycle of bison almost ended in extinction. Humans killed many bison in a short time, and new bison were not being born fast enough to replace the animals that were killed.

A difficult beginning

Sea turtles are having difficulty keeping their life cycle going. They nest on sandy beaches, and there are only a few suitable ones left. People disturb or destroy the nesting sites by building tourist resorts along the beaches. Some predators dig up and eat the eggs. If any survive long enough to hatch, crabs and gulls often eat the tiny turtles as they travel over the beach from their nest to the ocean.

On their own, few baby turtles are able to complete their journey across the beach.

*Some sea turtles are **endangered**, or in danger of dying out. To help the turtles, scientists take eggs from the beaches and care for them in a warm, safe place. After the turtles hatch, they are taken back to the beaches and released in the ocean.*

Words to know

embryo A living thing in the early stage of its life, before it is born, hatched, or sprouted

exoskeleton A hard covering on the bodies of some animals

extinct Describing a plant or an animal that no longer exists

fungus A living thing, including a mushroom or a mold, that gets food from plant and animal matter

gill A body part that fish and other water animals use in order to breathe

larva A baby insect, fish, or amphibian after it hatches from an egg; a larva has a soft, wormlike body

life cycle The stages in the life of a living thing from birth to reproduction

live born Describing an animal that is born alive from its mother's body

lung One of usually two body parts that most animals use to breathe air

mate To join together to make babies

metamorphosis The major change in appearance and behavior that some animals go through between birth and adulthood

nutrient A substance that living things need for growth and good health

offspring The young of a living thing

placenta The organ through which unborn mammal babies receive food and oxygen from their mothers' bodies

pollution Harmful materials, such as waste or garbage, which can make the Earth unclean

reproduce To make offspring

species A group of closely related living things that can have babies with one another

sperm A male reproductive cell that joins with a female's egg to make babies

tadpole A baby amphibian that lives underwater and breathes with gills

yolk The part of an egg that provides food for the growing embryo

Index